The A to Z Book
of
Endangered Animals

Written by Tammy Wunsch

Illustrated by Tammy Wunsch & ChatGPT

The A to Z Book
of
Endangered Animals

To the curious young explorers of our world, may this book inspire you to cherish and protect the magnificent creatures that share our planet. Your wonder and compassion can lead to great adventures and even greater acts of kindness towards all living beings. Let's journey together to learn, love, and save our animal friends before it's too late. Remember, even the smallest acts of care can make the biggest difference in their world—and ours.

A
is for
Amur
Leopard

Amur leopards live in the forests of Eastern Russia and China. They like to eat deer and small animals. Amur leopards can live up to 10-15 years. They are very good climbers and can run fast.

B
is for
Black
Rhino

Black rhinos live in Africa, in places with trees and bushes. They eat leafy plants and like to munch on branches. Black rhinos can live up to 35-50 years. They have two horns on their noses.

C
is for
Cheetah

Cheetahs live in the grasslands of Africa. They are super fast and eat animals like gazelles. Cheetahs can live up to 10-12 years. They have spotted fur and are the fastest land animals.

D
is for
Dugong

Dugongs live in warm sea waters near places like Australia. They eat sea grass on the ocean floor. Dugongs can live up to 70 years. They are big and gentle sea animals

E
is for
Emperor
Penguin

Emperor penguins live in Antarctica, where it's very cold. They eat fish and squid. Emperor penguins can live up to 20 years. They are the tallest of all penguins.

F
is for
Fin
Whale

Fin whales live in all the world's oceans. They eat small fish and tiny sea creatures called krill. Fin whales can live up to 90 years. They are very large, but swim fast.

G
is for
Gorilla

Gorillas live in the forests of Africa. They eat plants, fruit, and sometimes insects. Gorillas can live up to 35-40 years. They live in groups and are very strong.

H
is for
Hawksbill
Turtle

Hawksbill turtles live in tropical oceans around coral reefs. They eat sea sponges and can live up to 50 years. They have colorful shells and are good swimmers.

I
is for
Indochinese
Tiger

Indochinese tigers live in the forests of Southeast Asia. They eat animals like deer and wild boars. Indochinese tigers can live up to 15-20 years. They have beautiful stripes.

J
is for
Jaguar

Jaguars live in the rainforests and wetlands of Central and South America. Jaguars eat meat and are very strong hunters. They can live up to 12-15 years. Jaguars have beautiful spotted fur that helps them hide while they hunt.

K
is for
Kakapo

Kakapos are big, green, flightless birds that live in New Zealand. They eat seeds, fruits, and leaves. Kakapos can live up to 60 years. They are very rare and can't fly.

L
is for
Lemur

Lemurs live in forests on the island of Madagascar. Lemurs eat fruits, leaves, and sometimes insects. Lemurs can live up to 20 years. They have fluffy tails and big eyes that help them see in the dark.

M
is for Monarch Butterfly

Monarch butterflies live in North and South America. They eat nectar from flowers and milkweed plants. Monarch butterflies live up to a few months, but they travel very far.

N
is for
Narwhal

Narwhals live in the Arctic Ocean. They eat fish and squid. Narwhals can live up to 50 years. They have a long, spiral tusk, like a unicorn's horn.

O
is for
Orangutan

Orangutans live in the rainforests of Borneo and Sumatra. They eat fruit and leaves. Orangutans can live up to 30-40 years. They have long, red hair and are very smart.

P
is for
Pangolin

Pangolins live in Asia and Africa.
They eat ants and termites.
Pangolins can live up to 20 years.
They have scales on their bodies and
curl up into a ball when scared.

Q
is for
Quokka

Quokkas live on small islands off the coast of Western Australia. They eat plants and leaves. Quokkas can live up to 10 years. They are small, cute, and look like they are smiling.

R

is for

Red

Panda

Red pandas live in the mountains of Nepal and China. They eat bamboo and fruit. Red pandas can live up to 14 years. They have reddish-brown fur and a long, fluffy tail

S
is for
Saola

Saolas live in the forests of Vietnam and Laos. They eat leaves and plants. Saolas are very rare and not much is known about them, including their lifespan. They are sometimes called "Asian unicorns.

T
is for
Tasmanian
Devil

Tasmanian devils live in Tasmania, Australia. They eat meat and are scavengers. Tasmanian devils can live up to 6 years. They are black with a loud growl.

U
is for
Uakari

Uakaris live in the Amazon rainforest. They eat fruit, leaves, and insects. Uakaris can live up to 20 years. They have red faces and short tails.

V
is for
Vaquita

Vaquitas are small dolphins that live in the Gulf of California. They eat small fish and squid. Vaquitas can live up to 20 years. They are very rare and the most endangered marine mammal.

W

is for

Wolverine

Wolverines live in the cold forests and tundra of the Northern Hemisphere. They eat meat and are very strong. Wolverines can live up to 13 years. They are tough and have thick fur.

X

is for

Xingu

River Ray

Xingu River rays live in the Xingu River in Brazil. They eat small fish and insects. Not much is known about their lifespan. They are flat and live at the bottom of the river.

Y

is for
Yangtze
Finless
Porpoise

Yangtze Finless Porpoises live in the Yangtze River in China. They eat fish and shrimp and can live up to 20 years. They are playful but very rare.

Z
is for
Zebra
Shark

Zebra sharks live in the tropical oceans near coral reefs. They eat small sea animals. Zebra sharks can live up to 25-30 years. When they are young, they have stripes like a zebra.

Bonus
Endangered
Animals

S
is for
Snow
Leopard

Snow Leopards are big cats that live in the Asian mountain ranges. They eat wild sheep and goats and live from 10 to 12 years. Snow leopards can leap up to 50 feet in one jump.

P
is for
Panda

Giant **P**andas live in bamboo forests in central China and eat bamboo. They typically live around 20 years and have a pseudo-thumb, an extended wrist bone that helps them grasp and eat bamboo efficiently.

T
is for
Leatherback
Turtle

Leatherback **T**urtles live in the deep oceans around the world. They eat lots of jellyfish every day and can live up to 45 years. They are the largest sea turtles and can dive as deep as a tall building!

C
is for California Condor

California **C**ondors live in the rocky mountains and forests of California. They eat dead deer and cattle. These big birds can live up to 60 years. They have the largest bird wingspan in North America, stretching up to 9.5 feet wide!

P

is for Visayan Warty **P**ig

Visayan Warty **P**igs live in forests in the Philippines. They eat fruits, roots, and small animals. These pigs can live up to 10 years in the wild. The warty bumps on their faces protect them when they fight with other pigs.

C
is for Bactrian Camel

Bactrian Camels live in the Gobi Desert, where it's very dry. They eat grass and leaves and live up to 40 years. They have two humps that store fat to help them survive when there's not much food or water around.

Simple ways for YOU to help protect Endangered Animals?

1. Learn and Share: Find out cool facts about endangered animals and share what you learn with your friends and family. The more people know about these animals, the more they will want to help them too!
2. Recycle and Reuse: By recycling things like paper, plastic, and cans, and reusing items instead of throwing them away, we help keep the Earth clean. A cleaner Earth is a better home for animals!
3. Save Energy: Turn off lights, TVs, and computers when you're not using them. Saving energy helps fight climate change, which is important for keeping animals' homes safe.
4. Plant a Tree: Trees give homes to lots of animals and help clean the air. Planting a tree with your family can be a fun way to help animals and the planet.
5. Be Kind to All Animals: Remember, all animals are important, even the small ones like bugs and spiders. Being kind to them helps everyone live together happily.
6. Support Animal Sanctuaries: Visit or donate to animal sanctuaries or zoos that take care of endangered animals. Your support helps them keep these animals safe and healthy.
7. Beach and Park Clean-ups: Join local clean-up days at beaches, parks, or rivers. Keeping these places clean means animals have safer places to live.
8. Use Less Plastic: Try to use less plastic, like saying no to plastic straws and using reusable water bottles. Plastic can hurt animals, especially in the ocean.

Glossary:

Endangered animals are special friends in nature who don't have many family members left. It's like if you had a rare toy that few people have. We must care for them and their homes so they don't disappear forever. It's important to help them stay safe, happy, and healthy so they can have more family members and be around for a long time.